Sean O'Brien

November

PICADOR

First published 2011 by Picador
an imprint of Pan Macmillan, a division of Macmillan Publishers Limited
Pan Macmillan, 20 New Wharf Road, London N1 9RR
Basingstoke and Oxford
Associated companies throughout the world
www.panmacmillan.com

ISBN 978-0-330-54408-5 HB
ISBN 978-0-330-53500-7 PB

A CIP catalogue record for this book is available from
the British Library.

Printed in the UK by CPI Mackays, Chatham ME5 8TD

Visit **www.picador.com** to read more about all our books
and to buy them. You will also find features, author interviews and
news of any author events, and you can sign up for e-newsletters
so that you're always first to hear about our new releases.

For David and Julia

Contents

November

Fireweed

Look away just for a moment.
Then look back and see

How the fireweed's taking the strain.
This song's in praise of strong neglect

In the railway towns, in the silence
After the age of the train.

Jeudi Prochain

The Muse, your ex, Miss Jeudi Prochain,
Keeps all your pleading letters but reads none.
One day in someone else's mail you find
A postcard from the nineteenth century –
A train, some smoky poplars, sheds –
But she's already gone to spend the winter
Nursing Rilke in a Schloss. The gods themselves
Don't have her private number. You once did.

The markets crash and war breaks out.
Meanwhile the state is withering away,
Not that you'd notice, while she rides a tank
Bedecked with roses through the ruined capitals.
She understands why even thieves and murderers
Have their appeal – or so they care to think,
For whether they will hang, or go to ground
In Paraguay, is all the same to Miss Prochain.

You should not speak to her of history or taste,
Though she defines them both. No apparatus
Nails her to the scholar's inky sheets
But in her lightest moment she's more serious
Than Auerbach and Sophocles combined.
You never know, and yet you thought you did,
And here's your punishment, this hell of time
Unbroken by amnesia or lies.

She lets herself be photographed
In Hitler's bath — as though she'd even be
American, when truthfully, for Jeudi, terms
Like 'international' and 'cosmopolitan'
Are too parochial to suit the girl
Who in one instant shyly bleeds a pig
Beside a sunlit window in Provence
And next is all severity in furs.

When Lenin's train obligingly chugs in
Beside a snowbound halt near Riga,
Miss Prochain will prefer to board her own
Discreet express for Lhasa, there to watch
M. le Comte de St-Germain expire:
And yet this very evening, look, she leans upon
An attic windowsill in Paris and removes
A shred of dark tobacco from her lip,

And then Miss Jeudi sings, inaudibly,
To rainy slates where angel-chaperones of cloud
Have paused to smile on her, at an address
That you can see from here but never reach,
And where, as you alone will understand,
From now until the crack of doom
(Which naturally will not affect her plans)
Miss Prochain is unable to reply.

The Citizens

We change the river's name to make it ours.
We wall the city off and call it fate.
We husband our estate of ash,
For what we have we hold, and this
Is what is meant by history.
We have no love for one another, only uses
We can make of the defeated.
– And meanwhile you have disappeared
Like smoke across a frozen field.

What language? You had no language.
Stirring bone soup with a bone, we sip
From the cup of the skull. This is culture.
All we want to do is live forever,
To which end we make you bow down to our gods
In the midday square's Apollonian light
Before we ship you to the furnaces
And sow you in the fields like salt.

We fear that the fields of blue air at the world's end
Will be the only court we face.
We fear that when we reach the gate alone
There will be neither words nor deeds
To answer with. Therefore, we say, let us
Speak not of murder but of sacrifice,
And out of sacrifice make duty,
And out of duty love,
Whose name, in our language, means death.

Sunk Island

She stares down the dead straight mile, at a walk,
While I stand by the lych-gate to let her
Arrive at this slow-motion replay of England.
Can I help you? asks the lady on the horse.
And I don't say: too late, unless your powers include
Self-abolition. *Me? I'm waiting.* I don't say:
Leave me be to read your graves, to stand and think,
To hear the water taking back the frozen fields.

It's not my place to tell you what I mean.
Perhaps I've come to use the weather up
And look too closely at your groves of oak and ash.
But we both know the fact I'm waiting here
Is cousin to a crime. We hold each other's gaze.
Who for? her bladed helmet asks. Her horse has turned
To steaming stone. I think I hear the sea far off,
Like evidence that each of us might call.

And why? – For the flood to accelerate over this ground,
For your helmet to circle and sink like a moral,
For a rag-and-bone man with his cargo of trash
To come rowing past slowly, his mind given over
To practical matters, the pearls of your eyes
Unforgiven and sold at Thieves' Market
For sixpence and never once thought of again.
You must be cold out here, she says. I think I must.

Salisbury Street

Correct. You can't go back. But then we saw the gate,
Or where the gate had stood, and it was nothing much
To step on to the asphalt lawn, to try to find
The rise of the old terrace, or the vanished fountain's
Vanished pool, the stumps that had been walnut trees,
Then slide down mounds of landfill to the orchard.

It was easy, standing in the wreck. The ragged elder-clumps
Had driven out the rest, except the cherry tree,
And that was sick with creepers. She was curious
To reach the very end, but I could see from there
The Bramley by the wall was gone, and in its place
A shed had fallen on itself and left a chair to wait.

The earth was pitted, friable, confused
With plastic sheeting, concrete, poisoned grass and rugs,
The inability to concentrate or care. Suppose
There'd been mosaics: someone would have made a point
Of shitting on them, when they'd burnt the books.
But it was nothing personal. Who were we, anyway?

These woods had held their own blue light, serene interiors
For autumn days like this, but now they stank –
Stale milk and burning mattresses. Smoke hung like ignorance.
You might have thought the place had always been like that,
A ruined grove of raw tin tongues, a sacred site
For drunks' amnesia and suicide. You can't go back.

Josie

I remember the girl leaning down from the sunlight
To greet me. I could have been anyone. She could not:
She was Josie, remember, and smiling – she knew me already –
Auburn gate-girl to the garden-world,
To the lilacs and pears, the first summer
Seen perfectly once, then never again. And she left.
The garden – the garden, of course, has gone under the stone
And I cannot complain, a half-century gone
Like the cherry tree weeping its resin,
The dry grass, the slab of white marble
The butcher propped up in the back yard to sit on –
Things of the world that the world has no need of,
No more than of Josie or me or that morning.
Still a child as I see now, she leaned down
To smile as she reached out her brown hands to greet me
As though this were how these matters must be
And would be forever amen. She was saying goodbye.
And I cannot complain. What is under the stone
Must belong there, and no voice returns,
Not mine and not hers, though I'm speaking her name.

Verité: Great Junction Street

One weekday afternoon when we are dead,
We will be readmitted here for free –
Phantoms of sweat and smoke and ash,
Yet honoured patrons – to a special
Double feature that eventually
Begins with *Pearl and Dean*: *Complete*.
Back then we never saw the point
Of blotchy tedium and jaundiced lights,
And did not wish to live in nineteen fifty-eight
Among stiff perms and brilliantine and breath.
We had ideas, or we had hopes,
Beyond our meagre competence.
We could not see that what the adverts meant
Was us, the grubby herd among the stalls.
The sprauncing morons and fat girls
Who lusted for a Hillman Minx were those
We'd marry: these must be the photos –
See us grimacing with happiness
While two dogs copulate discreetly
Underneath a well-placed knacker's van.
Be silent, please. Watch closely. Now
Bite down, once more, my fellow citizens, into
The silver foil in which your choc-ice comes,
For when it meets your fillings that is all
The ecstasy eternity will grant –
No tongues, no hands up skirts, no chance.
And next, as if this were not quite enough,

Sit back to relish *Look at Life:*
The North Norwegian Lamprey Trade.
Somehow we must have missed it first time round.

After the painting Great Junction Street *by Jock McFadyen*

Cahiers du Cinema

As though between performances, the 'varnished waves' of
seats are gone,
Their dreaming space abolished with those darkened afternoons
Spent sunk in sticky ginger plush, revising *The Belles of*
St Trinian's
Or *The Three Hundred Spartans*, with David Farrar (Xerxes)
Sulking on his golden catafalque, his voice of cold command
Not only underused but dubbed for overseas. The end.
In Purgatory, that crawling corridor where we are only ever
Halfway up the queue, there will be questions asked, of course.
Herr Oberst, I can only tell you what I know: Karl Malden
And his hooter sniffed out Robert Shaw and all his Tigers
Camouflaged beneath the snows of the Ardennes. A dirty war,
When even Bronco Layne's a Nazi in disguise. Does any of
this count
When the space closes into itself, the shadows go back in
the box
And the box into nothing? In place of memory, 'dark nostalgia'.
Bah.

A poster in a newly opened shop professes to preserve
A thing you never thought you'd need to own. You must
           re-learn
The dreaming gaze that formerly you aimed with gluttonous
            indifference
At anything and everything that now you cannot prove
           was once
The past, in all its posthumous authority, plus free mistakes.
Begin with August's dusty cumulus at five o'clock, when you
And all the other creeps and criminals emerged unwillingly
Into the orange glare of actuality, to find the city charged
           once more
With an intolerable tedium whose grammar could not house
Your guilty joys. Oh, Natalie, *en deshabille*, detained by
           grim hussars
While climbing from a bosky pool in far Bohemia, somewhere
The glinting Tony Curtis, even, might not rescue you!
On one hand there were things the lard-faced devotee might
           have absorbed
Officially (the 'facts'), and then there was the world, e.g.

This dark-eyed goddess, warm as breath, remote as a Czarina.
Forget the school of life: post-cinematic sadness taught me all
                                                    I know,
For instance that a man may have to choose between a woman
And a train, and even though she's Jeanne Moreau, who makes
The glummest scullery an everywhere, the outcome's black
                                                    and white,
And off limps Burt to keep his date with the *chemin de fer*,
To take revenge for Dufy and for France, for Papa Boule
                                            (Michel Simon)
Shot out of hand by Wolfgang Preiss quite early on behind
                                            the engine shed.
'If we are to live, then let us live,' Kirk Douglas might have
                                                    screamed,
Anachronistically, but he preferred to dance along the oars.
We all know men like that, oppressively ebullient, but which
                                                    of us
Knows Janet Leigh, so strangely underdressed for her excursion
On the longship? And who else dare wave her past but Poitier
                                            and Widmark,
Delighted by distraction from their own marine catastrophe?

Farewell, supreme foyer where it was always afternoon!
Arriving in the middle I could always leave when I came in,
Collapsing time into the image of an arrow shower
Curving out of sight, as in *The Charge at Feather River* –
Modernism, yes, but this was Hull: no 3D specs for us.
There in the silence between features, perching on a
                                        crumbling ledge
Above the gulfs and Thrones and Dominations of the grim
                                        Criterion
I wondered at the vast occluded system of the secondary stars,
Calhoun and Madison, Mahoney, Chandler, Aldo Ray and
                                        Gordon Mitchell,
Rough riders–Tarzan–beefcake–stuntmen and in Mitchell's case
Achilles, grieving, very slowly, at the pyre of Patroclus, when
                                        all at once
The credits rolled, the lights came up and here was that
                                        unnatural act,
An end without a settlement of blood. The gods themselves
Were tired, like the furniture of heaven. Outside the streets
                                        were dark.

– Dark as Edgar Wallace in his Albany of death. On every floor
A crew was grimly working to supply the second feature,
Like Catholics persisting in the forms when faith was gone
To frame an image of an underfunded English Purgatory
Complete with acts and fatal outcomes but with nobody to care.
– And yet one afternoon you wake to find yourself in Finland
Kissing Françoise Dorléac in her tiny knitted dress, and as
                                                              she feels
To find the space between your vertebrae and with the other
                                                              hand
Extracts a hatpin from the mattress, it is clear that you will
Live forever. It is snowing. As the Gulf of Riga drinks down
General Midwinter's army, then locks itself with ice once more,
Then, English, Colonel Stok observes, *you have no choice except
                                                              to live
Forever*. It is snowing. Kiss her. It is snowing. Kiss the girl
And soon you will no longer know the blizzard from the screen.

– O Muse of Cinema, who taught us waking sleep, who warned
And guided with your sudden torch, and served us food
Intended for the undecaying teeth of gods, I think I saw
                                                    you once
In mortal form, far down the long red corridor, with one hand
                                                    cupped
Beneath your elbow as the other raised a cigarette, while you
                                                    stared up
Into the smoke as though just then you longed to be like one
                                                    of us,
To give back your omniscience and lounge at prayer with all
The other ladies at the matinee, with drunks and desperate
                                                    old men
And games-evading schoolboys, all of those who shared a faint
And yet abiding sense that what was shown might prove to be
A trailer for the life to come, when all the Forms from slapstick
Through to evil via Rin Tin Tin and Vera Ellen would at last
Unmask themselves, and with our watching brief fulfilled
We'd make our way in silence through the exits into perfect
                                                    nonexistence.

But all this has been stolen – all the light, these dustmotes in
                                                        the beam,
The self-forgetfulness and boredom and desire, headache,
                                                        toothache,
Arse-ache, blessed privacy, these visions in the isolation tank
Of borrowed afternoons that for some unknown reason never
                                                        found
Their way back into rightful ownership by idiots and bores.
                                                        Till now.
Now is the victory for common sense, and those of us
                                                who spent our youth
In thrall to the delirious excrescences of self-consuming Kapital
Will have to find another means by which to cross the
                                                        shadow-line
That separates Hilts from Switzerland, and Gina Lollobrigida
                                                        from almost
All her clothes. We watchers in the cave are cast out once for all
Into that fearful teatime light where everything is being filmed
And narrative has given way entirely to its critics, who
                                                        must read
A thousand screens at once for damning evidence of dreams.
We will confess to everything except the present tense.

White Enamel Jug

The Ardennes

There used to be a white enamel jug,
Its rim precise in Prussian blue –
Likewise the handle with its female curve
Through which a forage cap might fit: the jug
The maid's deserter drank from, slowly,
Boots off, his feet on the kitchen table,
Raising the thing like a trophy over his head
And licking his white cat-moustache,
While she kept waiting, trying not to laugh
At what a crime it was, behind him
In the doorway, naked, with her hand stretched out.
Midnight was all the time there was.
The stars froze, branches creaked, the cream
Sank in the jug, and so they took their happiness
For there and then and not for memory:
As, in his way, the Major also did
When he had sent his manservant to bed
And poured black coffee from this jug,
Then sat to write the letter home,
But paused, as though to read his palms
Within the circle of the lantern, while the jug
Attended, patiently, a kind of company
The night the war was lost, before
He rose and at the window watched the dark
Until at dawn the forest turned to flame.

Sleep

Like youth, this language has forgotten you.
Lost on the tip of its tongue, you could wait
A long time to be missed. Get up and read:
A poem, the Bible, a *roman policier*, *Hello!*
Or the blank white back of the bathroom door.
Some never lose the ear of sleep. They switch
Like diplomats descending aircraft steps
Into the lingua franca with a yawn,
But – you know who you are – you're too ashamed
At your incompetence to even share
A mason's grip: you lie there making do,
Until the clock itself nods off at last,
While every failure brings you its account
For signing, every sin its sweat, each gaffe
Its slo-mo loop for fresh analysis.
You sleepless masses, whither politics?
Your *Marseillaise* must be *Lillibulero*,
Daybreak more Dunkirk than Alamein.
At last, the drivel of unfree association
Trails you through the endless day, where you must
Imitate the living to the letter, dying
For a pod to come for you like all the rest
To snatch your sleeping body for rebirth,
However brutal the regime might prove.
You would run howling down the alleyways
In packs, to trap the rotten elements –
Your former self included, naturally –

And tear them limb from limb,
From pitiless necessity do anything
So long as you need never wake again.

Europeans

Now we are in Europe let us take
To selling mushrooms by the roadside,
Broad-brimmed platefuls and uniform buttons
Plucked before dawn in the forest of birch,
The dank delicious one-legged flesh
Climbing from grave-pits as big and as deep
As the forests themselves, for it does not
Take long to establish the custom, not long
To forget the beginning, to hold up
A bucket or basket of mushrooms
And talk about always and offer a shrug
That proves our knowledge and our ignorance
Identical, proverbial, entirely
Beyond the scope of history or law,
And since we have always been here
On our fold-away chairs near the crossroads,
Hunched in black overcoats, pale as our produce,
Seeking and selling the flesh of the earth
By the handful and kilo in brown paper bags,
We cannot be other than real.

Elegy

Just round a corner of the afternoon,
Your novel there beside you on the bed,
Your spectacles to mark your place, the sea
Just so before the tide falls back,
Your face will still be stern with sleep

As though the sea itself must satisfy
A final test before the long detention ends
And you can let the backwash take you out.
The tall green waves have waited in the bay
Since first you saw the water as a child,
Your hand inside your father's hand, your dark eyes
Promising you heartbreak even then.
Get on with it, I hear you say. *We've got no choice.*

We left the nursing home your tired chair.
They stole the sweets and flowers anyway
And bagged your clothes like rubbish in the hall.
Here in the flat your boxed-up books and ornaments
Forget themselves, as you did at the end.
The post still comes. The state that failed to keep the faith
Pursues you for its money back. *There's nothing worse,*
You used to say, *than scratting after coppers.*
Tell that to the clerks who'd rob your grave,
Who have no reason to remember how
You taught the children of the poor for forty years
Because it was the decent thing to do.

It seems that history does not exist:
We must have dreamed the world you've vanished from.
This elegy's a metaphysical excuse,
A sick-note meant to keep you back
A little longer, though you have no need to hear
What I must say, because your life was yours,
Mysterious and prized, a yard, a universe away.

But let me do it honour and repay your gift of words.
I think of how you stared into the bonfire
As we stood feeding it with leaves
In the November fog of 1959,
You in your old green coat, me watching you
As you gazed in upon
Another life, a riverside address
And several rooms to call your own,
Where you could read and think, and watch
The barges slip their moorings on the tide,
Or sketch the willows on the further shore,
Then in the evening stroll through Hammersmith
To dances at the Palais. *Life enough*,
You might have said. *An elegant sufficiency.*
There was a book you always meant to write.

You turned aside and lit a cigarette.
The dark was in the orchard now, scarf-soaking fog
Among the fallen fruit. The house was far away,
One window lit, and soon we must go back
For the interrogation to begin,
The violence and sorrow of the facts
As my mad father sometimes dreamed they were
And made the little room no place at all
Until the fit was past and terrible remorse
Took hold, and this was all the life we had.

To make the best of things. Not to give up.
To be the counsellor of others when
Their husbands died or beat them. To go on.

I see you reading, unimpressed, relentless,
Gollancz crime, green Penguins, too exhausted
For the literature you loved, but holding on.
There was a book you always meant to write
In London, where you always meant to live.
I'd rather stand, but thank you all the same, she said,
A woman on the bus to Hammersmith, to whom
I tried to give my seat, a woman of your age,
Your war, your work. We shared the view
Of willowed levels, water and the northern shore
You would have made your landing-place.
We haven't come this far to give up now.

The Lost Book

Here's where the far-gone Irish came to die
And having died got up to disappear
Into the space they wore into the air:
Smoke-room, bookies, God knows where –
They were a crowd who favoured solitude.
They came 'pro tem' and stayed, and stayed,
Bed-sitting room remittance-men
Whose files authority had usefully mislaid.
Dug out of 'kiln-baked' tombs, the gas left on,
This Tendency the calendar forgot
Kept suitcases of ancient paperwork
That could have grassed them up but didn't talk.
Poor demi-felons, dead of what? – of afternoons,
Whose rag and bone the council boxed and burned:
And you were of their party, were you not?

I owe you this. I watched you and I learned.
You lived provisionally, 'the man with no home team'.
Reliant on the Masonry of drink, you made
A modest and convincing entryist of crowds
Who only ever knew your Christian name,
Your trebles at Uttoxeter, perhaps
Your politics, on no account your game.
You seemed composed entirely of words.
'Tell no man – still less a woman – who you are.'
Who cares, now that the principals are dead
As the impossible morality

Whose prohibitions brought your lie to life
And in the end would send you off your head?
I care, for I was made to care.
You told a priest but couldn't tell your wife.
You were the author and the patient too,
And in another life another house
Imprisoned others and the clock had stopped.

You knew – and all you did was know –
That there was an appointment to be kept.
That was your art – to frame your punishment –
An endlessly extended sentence,
Solitary confinement in plain sight,
Nothing you could put down on the page,
Nothing you could ever simply name
But manifest in jealousy and rage
And episodes of heartbroken repentance.
There was nothing that could ever put it right.

'Yourself's a secret thing – take care of it,
But if it comes to handy grips you take no shit.'
Yours was a way of waiting, though you knew
That really there was nothing down for you
But vestibules and corridors and days
In which to seek permission to be old.
Kardomah Lampedusa, minus book,
Deported from successive realms of gold –
Longpavement and the Bronx and Hammersmith –
Or so you said, and who was I to ask?
Then when at last I came to take a look,

When you had sat it out as far as death,
Inside the case, behind the broken lock,
There were no secrets waiting underneath,
Just fragments of a poem you'd recite,
And scraps of stories you'd begun and re-begun,
In which the names alone would change, as though
You had forgotten who they were.

I found no history in this, no hidden world
Before I came – I'd heard your stuff bashed out
Through years of chainsmoked afternoons
And read it when you asked me to. I liked
The one where in the fog the sergeant found
His constable nailed up across a five bar gate,
But feared and did not understand the priest
In his deserted parish (fog again)
Who found his name had changed to Lucifer.
He lost his way and then he lost his mind
And that was that, with nowhere left to go,
Hell being where and who and what he was,
A state with neither origin nor end.

'The duty is to entertain,' you said, 'or else
To seek to make no sense at all.' And then
When you had filled the room with ash and smoke
There would be racing or the news, a second
Scouring of the *Telegraph*, a third, and no
Persuading you that you should persevere.
You were already old. Was that the plan?
To climb into the box and disappear

In smoke above the crematorium
And leave your furious pursuers unappeased
And shorn of purpose, standing in the snow
Beside the hearse, in mourning for themselves?

I studied you before the lid was sealed
And, as my mother had requested, placed
Rosemary for remembrance in your hands.
The deep, unhappy brow, the cloud-white hair
Combed back – oh, you were otherwise engaged.
In settling debts, or simply free to dream?
You wouldn't care to comment 'at this stage'.
Was there another world, where you belonged,
Or one more corridor where you still sit, rereading
With the patience of a lifetime
Last week's paper, hoping it might yield
To scrutiny and show the outcome changed?

Novembrists

This must be where I came in, gaberdined
Against the fog but part of it, to take the dark air,
Strolling on the glistening concrete of a tenfoot
When walking at night would be legal,
Which puts us somewhere in the nineteen fifties,
Entering the vast and ramifying silence
Issued by these garages and sheds that no one
Would think to repair or improve on. I admit
This is a version of the public good
Unthinkable to those not largely dead –
Those to whom a place is only somewhere on the way
To the apotheosis of transactions,
Those who fear the name Novembrists
And cannot see the point of it and in the end
Will probably decide they must forbid it,
Those who think that sentences like this
Should always finish with the number
Of a helpline, not more walking in the dark.
Here as we take the foggy night we hunger for it still,
And for the shoals of yellow leaves that come to rest
Beside a fallen fence where we can watch
The rabbi in his kitchen drinking tea alone.
Or Winifred Ratcliffe, teacher of pianoforte,
Staring back into a future from which she
Like us has vanished. She will make no sign:
We are Novembrists, are we not?
Reactionary elements combining in the dark

To undermine the decent light of trade
With futile knowledge of the spirit's appetite
For somewhere in between this world
And its discarded shadows. O Novembrists!
At the year's death, walking to no purpose
But to walk, among the rutted leaves
And dripping hawthorns, in behind
The sleeping yards and flooded lawns
And air-raid shelters piled with mattresses and comics,
Now I see it is my parents that I walk beside,
Her headscarf and his muted cigarette,
The desultory familiar talk, whose virtue
Lies in its routine, because it so
Resembles happiness we do not ask
For more, but only wish the night could be
Extended for an hour or a minute, though we know
The rules and limitations of November's paradise
And would not think to break them now
When not a bomb has fallen on the city
In a decade, and there is more or less
Enough to eat, and there are books at home.
I see the crime of this is modesty. I see
We should not universalise
A simple preference for foggy lanes
And intermittent lamp-posts, should not fall
Into the habit of the law, whose works
Are everywhere about us: and yet
Novembrists do not care to be
Entirely reasonable now. Come, then,
Fog and drizzle, frost and cigarettes

And dank austerity and blessed peace!
We merely wish the times, the state,
The market and the world and all
Their miserable implications could be brought
To silence for a moment by attending
Not to our unquantifiable delights
But closely to some business of their own.

Counting the Rain

Check the gas and hide the back door key.
Lock up. Make sure you have, and then
Go out and count the rain, and this time
Do it properly. You won't be home again.

The Plain Truth of the Matter

There are two tribes this world can boast —
The Marmite-lovers and the damned.
Fact is, though, everybody's toast,
Whatever breakfast they've got planned.

It's not for us to turn away
The sort who shun the dark-brown jar,
But sure as sure come Judgement Day
The Lord will know who His folk are.

First Time Around

You could make me believe with your fine tongue
That the sun rose in the west

I watch you cross the park out of the light,
At evening, for the sun falls in the East

To meet a pool of fire in the drain
Three streets away. It's me you're looking for.

The nuns at the French Convent disapprove.
Now Madam, where's your hat? Too short, the skirt.

Your life is not yet touched by mine –
The sun won't burn, the moon won't mask

And we must rule this kingdom as we wish –
These propped-up house-ends, bombsites,

Terraced lairs beneath the goods embankment.
Quickly, kiss me. Lie here. Learn to be imperious.

Sunday in a Station of the Metro

The pillars in the ruined church of steam
Reach up to rusty curlicues, whose branching forms
Once forged a second nature out of industry,
A forest where the wolves and Ridinghoods
Could figure both as cast and audience:
Victorian erotica on fire, with services
In both directions every twenty minutes.
Now through this sticky wood of suicides
Come morons and their monster dogs
To do their stint of shouting for tonight.

I fold my paper, turn it in my hands
Like a petitioner, and wait, and stare
Into the tunnel whose black throat
Is always on the brink of the oracular.
Brick-bowelled city, we would have a sign!
Should we applaud and go, or should we kneel
Inside the squares of light thrown down
Through broken sections of the roof?
How to appease or even wake the deity
From brick and iron and this evening-afternoon?

Is time still on the ration? More and more
I am inclined to do what everything
At once proposes and forbids. You, sir,
Dark-lantern man slipped out of time,
You with your skinny Eileen in your wake,
Take off your broken topper, shoot your dog
And look at me, as I break every
By-law known to God or man, walk slowly
To the platform's end, step down and then am seen
To vanish in the tunnel's mouth. As if.

Marine Siding

The final rusty flourish of the mountain ash
As it docks in a shower of sparks

At the scrapyard where railways and oceans
Merge at nowhere's entrepôt –

My friend, this is the famous happiness,
An alloy of the daylight world!

Closed

No cigarettes tonight. No tea. The spoon
Swings on a chain from the counter's edge.
Every cup and saucer's full of ash.
The buffet is pretending to be closed.
Inside it, under glass, a sandwich waits for you.
Stay here too long and it may speak your name.
The revels are but lately ended, bab.
You thought you understood austerity –
But fuck your sympathy and go without.
The white-tiled Gents is like a ruined temple.
Now it takes the democratic piss,
And would you care for a discreet disease?
What day it is. What time it is. What sea-coast
And what realm is this. The roof
Upheld by iron trunks, the arches uttering
New arches, further demarcations of
The darkness in the ramifying dark. The chance
That this might be the secondary place, that home
Lies just across the footbridge, through an arch,
Along a platform looking up and down
The ordinary night – and *there,* a steamy door,
Change counted out in halfpennies, received
With patience and a joke that no one but
The waitress and her pink-necked soldier hear.
You had to be there, you suppose. You never were.
It's in the way you tell 'em, in the fact
You know so well what you could never find.

The Island

Our island is full of detectives,
Believers in crime whose churches are stations.
See, they urge the engines on to justice
Down the slow branches of Sunday.
Abolished county towns
And ports deserted by the sea
And government establishments
On islands of their own on little lakes in woodland –
Bring them the gospel, detectives! By rail!

Who killed the White Horse?
The Long Man? Who severed his member?
Who did for the greenhouse? Who thrashed
The recalcitrant carpet to death
With a length of malacca?
Who commanded the hideous
Stockbroker villas be flung up like sets
For the Bad British Movie, redeemed
To a certain extent by the actors?

Perhaps we shall never be told –
For these are perfect murders, every one,
Yet our tireless detectives persist,
For example: the Jesuit literary critic,
His cursing-equipment concealed
In a modest valise; or the subaltern
Suddenly shell-shocked to forty,

Flinching in the ceaseless rain of limbs;
And the straight-talking lesbian polymath,
Clamped like a vice to the slightest evasion –

All have their says, taking turns
By the library fire on Sunday,
Or, weather permitting, outside on the lawn
As the fountains play over the pond
Where the dead in their green rooms look up
With expressions of genuine interest
As if this were something they might like
To read about properly later.

Where else could they possibly live,
Those who speak in that language
And gather in galleries, mourning themselves
In the work of Ravilious?
They are in the other country,
The place you might reach if you found
The right door and went in
To be treated as if you belonged
And heard yourself talk like a native
To summon a grey English beauty
From short afternoons, to be sure
How to live and believe
In the dark, near a railway.

Railway Lands

Over these moss-padded sleepers
The nineteenth century runs out of steam.
One rail vanishes, then both are imprints,
And next silver birches advance
Up the road from the other direction.
Yet people think this place has finished with itself:
An end to hawthorn, bindweed, brambles' practicality,
The accidental forest after work.
But here a level-crossing gate
Dividing nowhere off from nowhere else
Is losing its colour and pith in the rain
To the task of reversion, this sweet degradation,
Its O of red warning weathered into art
Among these labyrinthine galleries.
How shall we live, if not in this green anarchy?

If they take this there will be nowhere left,
No one to visit the turntable pit
For the fireweed rearing from oil-sweat,
To peer into the Marmite pools
For railway fish, no one to lie at dusk
Beneath cow parsley when it tilts
Its dishes to interrogate the moon,
No one to see the place become
Itself now that the meaning's gone.
It is as if we never lived, my love,
And never lay here afterwards
Where language takes its rest.
Where are you now?
Whose is this face I see
Inside the rusty water, just about to speak?

Infernal

It strikes you: you are here. It's quite a sight –
The pitchblack blazing lake of Hell by night
(The postcards stole their ancient joke from Hull).
And all alone, although it must be full.
There must have been a mixup on the quays –
You told them but the staff weren't listening.
Teabreak's over, lads – back on your knees.
All hail the chief. Prepare to kiss the ring.

Bruges-la-Morte

Suppose you lived in Bruges-la-Morte: this brown murk
would be blue –
Whistlerian the crepuscule, canals as thick as glue.

There to usurp the half-life led by M. Rodenbach,
Complete with thousand-metre stare and wispy ginger 'tache,

Your mission would be seeking out the Quartier Perdu –
A graveyard in a graveyard in the wake of Waterloo.

The beer would turn to incense. Demons would attack.
You'd escape from the asylum. They would come and fetch
you back.

You'd be an ultra-Catholic and worship Satan too,
Then form the object of a cult whose devotee was you.

With the national question looming you'd anticipate Degrelle,
But survive beneath the floorboards as a dark traditional smell,

A victim of the plot against the beautiful and true:
Next time, you'd say, *next time we'll know exactly who to screw.*

The verses you composed would neither edify nor please
And slowly you'd succumb to an unspecified disease –

The doctors would allege it was *nostalgie de la boue*
But they'd be sick themselves and there'd be nothing they
could do –

The fruit of pork and chocolate and aesthetic overdose,
Designed to prove that in the end all flesh is adipose.

Mud gave us Maeterlinck and Rops and (almost) you-know-who,
But rest assured that nobody would ever hear of you.

As you stared up through the sewage, black swans would stare
back down:
If you could speak you would declare that it's your kind
of town –

O Bruges-la-Morte! The sea itself has offered its adieux.
Whistlerian the crepuscule. Canals as thick as glue.
The streets are safe. No danger here of stumbling on The New.

The Drunken Boat

after Rimbaud

The vast indifferent river carried me, and in a while
The cries of sailors faded with the whoops of Seminoles
Who'd caught my crew and nailed them Roman-style
In decorative rows on totem poles.

Weighed down with Flanders wheat and English cotton,
I was of course untroubled by their fate.
Their cries were gone and they were soon forgotten,
And as the waters quickened I took flight.

Last winter in the furious beating of the seas,
While growing deafer than an infant's brain,
I ran! And the unmoored peninsulas
Were all seduced by chaos, so they won't be home again.

When I awoke at sea I had the blessing of the tempest.
Lighter than a cork I set off dancing on the surge,
The ever-rolling graveyard where the drowned may never rest.
Some put their faith in harbour lights: I never felt the urge.

The green sea found its way inside my hull of Swedish pine.
It was sweeter than the oozing flesh of windfalls to a boy,
And as it swabbed the decks of stains from puke and sour wine,
It also swept the rudder and the anchor-chain away.

Since when I have been bathing in the Poem of the Sea,
Infused with galaxies, lactating, drinking down
Green-azure, watching now and then, like flotsam drifting by,
A long-dead sailor turn in sleep and dream that he will drown.

Out here before your eyes the blue will drain out of the sea
When slow delirious rhythms working underneath
The glow of dawn, too strong for drink or poetry,
Ferment red love, more bitter on the lips than death!

I have seen waterspouts, seen lightning murdering the sky,
Seen undertows and currents and the evening's crepuscule,
Seen dawn's exalted race of doves set free to fly
And I have sometimes seen what men imagine to be real.

I have seen the low sun smeared with mystic horrors,
Projecting vast illusions on a screen of purple-grey;
Meanwhile the shutters of the waves, a Sophoclean chorus,
Beat and beat into the distance but will never get away.

I have dreamed the green night blinded by the snows,
Dreamed a kiss that rises slowly to meet the ocean's eyes
While sperm and ichor circulate on currents no one knows,
And dreamed the phosphor singing blue and yellow as the
                                        sun begins to rise.

For months on end I've followed where the swells
Stormed at the reefs like herds of maddened cattle in a pen,
Never dreaming that the Virgins' shining feet could quell
So suddenly the uproar of the ocean.

I have collided, I would have you know, with fabulous bayous
Where panthers go disguised in human skins,
Inseparable from flower-heads, while arching watergaws
Extend their underwater reins for anything with fins.

I have watched the fermentation of immeasurable mires
Where a complete Leviathan lay trapped among the rushes,
Seen water fall like stone upon flat calm from clear blue air
And distances sucked down into abysses!

And glaciers, silver sun and pearly waves and brazen skies,
Appalling landfalls in the depths of gulfs of ochre brume
Where serpents eaten from within by parasitic flies
Plunge from the twisted trees in clouds of black perfume.

I would have liked to show the children manatees
Born of the blue waves, the golden fish, the fish that sing.
Flowers of foam have rocked this argosy
And sometimes secret winds allowed me wings.

Sometimes, a martyr weary of the globe and north and south,
The sea whose lamentation sweetened my sea-road
Would offer me its shadow-flowers with yellow sucker-mouths
And like a penitent I knelt, and waited there and prayed . . .

I was almost an island. My walls were stucco'd with the crap
That pale-eyed fractious cackling sea-birds dripped.
When once more I went scudding on, across my ropes
Drowned men arose and then sank backwards into sleep.

Thrown by the hurricane into the birdless ether,
I, a vessel lost among the tresses of the coves,
I, whose sea-drunk carcass neither *Merrimack* nor *Monitor*
Nor Hanseatic brigantine would ever think to save;

Free and smoking, rising from the purple haze,
I who pierced the red sky like a wall beyond which can be got
A delicacy poets will be anxious to appraise
In which the lichens of the sun combine with sky-blue snot;

I who ran on, speckled with electric lunulae,
A raving plank, plus honour-guard of sea-horses in mourning,
When under hammer blows from cruel Julys
Blue heaven was a crater left perpetually burning;

I who trembled when I felt from fifty leagues away
The roar of rutting behemoths and tidal bores,
Interminable mover through blue immobility,
I yearn for Europe and her ancient belvederes.

I have seen star-archipelagos! And isles
Where the delirious skies lie open to the sailor. Can it be
That in those unfathomable nights you sleep your exile's
Sleep, O million golden birds, O power of futurity?

But truly I have wept too much, heartbroken by the dawn
And every cruel moon and bitter sun.
And love has bloated me with torpor. Oh, then,
Let my keel split and let me sink into the ocean.

Bathed in your weariness, O waves, I can no longer
Follow in the wake of cotton-boats, nor stand the brassy sulks
Of navies' flags and banners in the offing, nor
The dead-eyed gaze of loathsome prison-hulks.

If I long for European waters, it is for that pool,
Pitch-black and freezing, where at scented twilight
A child will come and crouch, brimful
With sorrows, and send out his fragile boat.

Michael

I see you often in your later phase –
A refugee from 1954,
Black-suited ascetic, destitute priest
With a flute in a carrier bag,
Having only the clothes you lay down in.

Today you stood among the crowds
Where Grafton Street meets College Green
And waited for the lights to change.
Do up your coat. And where's your scarf?
We don't want you to catch your death again.

The Landing-Stage

For Derek Mahon

Like one surprised yet tolerant,
You walk out of the darkness now
To speak to those you cannot see
Or quite believe in, though the place
Is stowed to bursting with the crowd
Who are, like foreign policy,
Especially concerned with you.

Now that you take the floor at last
We see it is a landing-stage, new-built
For the Odyssean returnee –
Port in a storm or final anchorage
No one can tell but you perhaps
Who even as you speak to us
Take care to keep your counsel still.

In our unheroic age
You have sustained a northern clarity
Enriched with the harmonics of the south,
And learned to voice whatever is the case
For wisdom's and its own sweet sake
As music, intimate and vast.
You let the grave itself unstop its mouth.

You tell the language that your love
Endures, whatever you have undergone
Of shipwreck or dry-docked disorder:
Wave-wanderer, beachcomber, far-flung
Singer with a shell for Nausicaa, at home
Nowhere and everywhere, but here and now,
And straddling the border once again.

Dinner at Archie's

i.m. Archie Markham 1939–2008

This place, the world, as you have more than once remarked,
More than once in fact tonight
Over this mound of roast lamb-with-no-veg and over the rim
                                             of your glass,

This world as we find it consists
Of two sorts of people: those here in the room and the rest,
On the one hand those present and then the great herd

Of the – how shall you put it – the *dim*
Who are not present to protest,
That one for instance, and *her*, and God help us, *him*;

Us and the rest, on the one hand the illuminati
And as you may at one time or another perhaps have remarked
The utterly and irredeemably endarked

Whom fortune and folly have somehow permitted
To be for the most part (catastrophically) in charge,
A theme upon which you are not normally slow to enlarge.

Have you mentioned this ever? Why, yes.
– Because, as you point out, coming back with more lamb
And in case there's a need an additional bottle of red,

It is of course something that every so often *needs* to be said,
And the likes of us – we happy few – have to come to the
help of the party,
Be it never so small and the truth elusive,

And expulsion – you look at me narrowly – rather more
likely than not,
While as for the others, at times they are almost enough,
One must confess, with their blather and rot,

To make one grow frankly abusive, alas,
And if that would be casting pearls before swine,
For example those toadies and gibbering no-marks in
Administration,

Well somebody's got to set an example and do it.
– And yet, though the day is sufficiently evil, no doubt
We shall somehow contrive to get through it

By means of a diet of lamb-with-no-veg and red wine,
Not to mention our native good humour
And sheer bloody genius, shan't we?

Of course we shall, Archie, of course,
For who could deny that it's fruitless to argue
With one like yourself who contrives to combine

The attributes of the immoveable object
With those of the irresistible force.
More lamb? More wine? No veg. Why, Archie, of course.

Porteriana

Transported back to demi-Paradise –
Via Port Said to aid comparison –
You note down all your city's names with care,
From Bongi-Bo to Heal's and Frognal (though
You draw the line at Haslemere), likewise
The Jacobean scorch-marks left
On pages from the *A–Z* where miniskirts
And lycanthropes have gone in hot pursuit
Of wisdom through the bars and galleries.
The ugly rich resemble gods; the poor
Are no one but themselves; the streets are paved
With unconsoling instances, and while you work
In that high room among the holy notes,
Between the rooftops dusk stands like belief
To lead us on but not to bear our weight.
Then there are landlords to be gratified.
In time all this will help compose
The epic Bach and Arthur Mee have hinted at.
The scratches on the ceiling of the tube,
Pontormo's murdered God, those things with shears,
The whole of death and loss, are to be reconciled
In 'music's huge light irresponsibility',
When in the garden in the square the dead
Are helped into the day and spoken with afresh
Across the long white tablecloths
Where bread and wine are eagerly supplied
By teams of deaf-mute journalists and critics. There

It will be always afternoon, the taxis purring
Calmly at the gates, the oratorio delighted
To possess its soul in patience, while inside the hall
The Berlin Philharmonic longs for your arrival.

Leavetaking

In memory of Peter Porter

In a draughty terrace bar
Beside the *cave* at Château Ventenac,
And lapped by the green Midi canal,
I take my leave, old friend,
By raising *une pression* and not
The Minervois that you would recommend.
Bad news prefers its poison cold and long.
The news has not improved so far –
So, keep the decent bottle in the rack
For later, for the 'decent interval'
That death like a bureaucracy requires.

Or maybe neck it in the midnight heat
Up at the house when everyone's in bed,
At one end of the huge white tablecloth,
At which a Nazi colonel also sat
To sample the warm south
While waiting for the war to end –
The kind of fact you would absorb
For later, but there is no later now.
Flute-playing psychopaths all must
Like cats and poets come to dust,
But I will not be reconciled.

The evening boats slide in,
Last autumn's leaves still piled
Along their guttering and in the seats
Of plastic chairs left out on deck
In token of a former merriment
In which I am required to believe
When the patron, a rugby star
From some time back, limps past
To put another freezing glass beside the last,
Then fire the oven up with grubbed-up vines
And stand admiring its crimson speech
As though like alcohol it were
A kind of poetry. My friend,
Is there sufficient detail for you yet?
You'd know much faster than I ever could
The point at which the orchestration starts
And evening is converted into art.

La patronne with her brutal crop
And wide-girl suit comes out
To criticize the styling of the blaze.
The grinning barman comes by bicycle
And finds their bickering, the bar,
The voices from the dim canal, the flicker
Of the bunting's spectral tricolores
A stage to serve his wordless drollery:
These are perhaps our characters, but where's
The crowd to fill the choruses
Of black-edged pastoral?

The world, you'd say, exists
Not to be understood
But to demand conviction. I assent,
As if it matters, and the dancers have arrived,
Cool, pink-pastelled blondes who
In another life have raised
A *parapluie* at Cherbourg, squired
By lupine George Chakirises in black.

This is the world, or part of it.
They do not think themselves Shakespearean,
Although you might, were we to sit
Beside the water here, me with *une pression*
And you among the quiet notes you will transform
Into a poem in the high nine hundreds.
I have not learned your lesson yet.
Work is good, like love and company,
But these so-courteous deaths, who sweep
Their maidens up and down the shore
In perfect silence on their light fantastic feet
(When did the music stop?) insist
That they are quite another thing,
Sent from a place less beautiful than this
But just as carefully designed,
The shade beyond the trees and the canal,
Where evening ends, and songs likewise,
And there is no one left to sing.

The Heat of the Day

Deep in the restaurant afternoon, we share
The hypnagogic drowse of smoking cooks,
Their seething pans, the far white gaze of fish
Awaiting resurrection by the night.
Some days we think at first it's tinnitus,
But then, for those civilians who can't take
The noise itself or face its jealous glare,
These proxies of the sun evoke our roaring star,
Its gold and black, its cruel command.
Cicadas have to scratch their itch en masse,
Each breath the friction of a Lucifer
Against the empyrean. Fuming skeletons
Botched up from old cicada-wrecks,
Then dipped in phosphorus and set ablaze
Before the god who never calls or writes,
No wonder if they're mad to keep the faith.
Like nudist zealots on the harbour wall
Who want their shadows scorched into the rock,
In time it might be possible to learn
How not to dwell on ice-cubes or the dark,
But atheists are indoors having sex
By thunderous air-con, while we're marooned
Beneath this blinding canvas, hard at work.
The sun is not quite real, nor this white heat,
Nor the cicadas in their adoration.
We're Northerners. We need rehearsals first,
Improving views of Hell from time to time,

The heat deferred into the grave, the fact,
We like to think, beyond imagining.
So then, let's drain this burning glass
And try with incandescent tolerance to catch
The waiter's lizard eye and beg a light –
A sip of petrol? No, but please, the bill,
Though our incinerated voices,
Flaring white with eager terror, sound
Far distant, like the tinnitus of gods.

Tables and Chairs

'the innocent walls and light'
Roy Fuller

The tables and chairs, 'the innocent walls and light',
Would be nowhere without us. Enter this house
At the edge of a field, where two unnumbered roads
Converge and part across a ridge of silver birch.
The mirrors and the ornaments survive
The almost-hush of the unopened air; the figures
In the photographs look back in smiling disbelief
From the Town Hall steps. Those were the days.
So what are these, these silences that never cease
To fall between darkness and darkness,
That we cannot interrupt with speech
Or gestures or routine or love? What shall we gain
By witnessing the pathos of a ewer
Standing in an old stone sink,
As faithful and attentive as a dog? If we should
Scrutinize the cracked glaze of a tile
Left lying on the window-sill, and then pass on
To emulate the windows' wall-eyed stare
At ordinary emptiness, a yard, the gate
Ajar to take us back where we began
And see us off the premises,
What margin of endurance do we think
We'll find, between necessity and chance?

Aspects of the Novel

1. Chapter 16

In which the action pauses for an hour
To let the characters rehearse their manias
And share a glass there in the poisoned glade.
Time passes? It does not. Time flies.
The reader cannot wait for homicide.
The danger is this may be only literature,
Whose love is all for means and never ends,
Whose very rhetoric confers
An immortality of sorts, a long
Engagement, not a zipless fuck.
But these are monsters we have come among.
A line of Nietzsche turns to three of coke,
To reminiscence. Anyone might think
Their past was real and likewise their regret
For everything that led them here
To this green silence (no birds sing) to drink
Gall to the lees and rave into the night.
Their leisure is an index of anxiety.
Their watches throb like ulcers. Sticky cushions
Rub against the women's legs. When can it be
If not tonight the worst suspicions
Voice themselves? If not tonight, when shall we
Care about these passions? Wait and see.
For him the problem is ontology, for her
The inability to read the signs that what

This evening holds must be a dripping axe,
And, for their friend, the difference
Between the crimson notion and the fact.
Time they were going, though, high time
We parted at the turning of the page
To meet our ignorance afresh,
And leave them in their papered catacomb
To lie and dream themselves awake, and yet
We wait, we wait, and evening turns to ash.

2. *Want of Motive*

You detect a want of motive here
But don't you find motive
Is what you become on the way,
O seeker after knowledge,
Truth and beauty, equipped
With disposable income? No?

Don't you sometimes find
That history's at work
In you as in the rest,
The living and the dead
And the imagined?
Or perhaps you don't.

Fare forward then, traveller!
Into the white-gold hinterland

Devoted to Apollo,
Right-angled rectitude
Clear sightlines, God's truth
And nobody, nobody there.

3. *The Uninvited Reader*

'There was no one I could identify with'

It was unwise to come here looking for a friend
Among the long-established enmities
Assembled on this summer night to mark
The marriage of the dim to the perverse
With shadowy foretelling and asides
Among the ha-has and the sheds:

For what this cast of characters requires
Is an audience, the formal kind
That servants or a governess would once supply –
The help, essential but unheard, their tiny love,
If love it was, less unrequited
Than ignored. You do know this?

Perhaps in fact it's why you came
And keep on coming, not so much to feel
That what you feel goes unrewarded as to learn
With a succinct, addictive pain, like so,
That here, since no one at the party cares,
It ceases to exist. Now get your coat.

The River on the Terrace

Time after time, the river of light
Flows down the broad steps of the terrace
Between the white walls and blue shutters

And under the carob and grapevine, coming on
In slow gold blinks, in indigo and rust,
Minting coins to sink among the shadows

It discards as it conceives them,
Folding clean sheets out of nothing,
Wheeling then pausing minutely as if

On the unbroken skin of itself.
Its depth is the authority it wields
To hold us to this wager, sliding past our feet

Over the plain of cracked paving-stones,
Onwards to the terrace-end, then out and down
Into the burning mezzogiorno air.

The river sinks into the rock. It never was,
Until a breeze comes up the valley
And the water re-awakes. Again we watch,

Like travellers halted at a ford,
Beside this force that seems to be anxiety.
What is it like, what is it like,

Unpassing epoch-afternoon, dry bed
Through which the river fades, then flows?
Like love, and like anxiety, like this.

Narbonne

The sound of a train is the sound of the wind
In the narrow streets, is nowhere, is a train
Not taken, though I see its swaying corridors
Framing the sun's flight second by second
And wake to a scattering of rain at the glass,
To streets I have been dreaming, still and wet,
From which the sound has only now
Yet therefore utterly departed, which is why
I go on listening anyway, until
The silence too exhausts itself and once again
The wind sings in the eaves and campaniles.
I know that when we lie at rest
You listen too, that you are not afraid
If clearly we shall have to live forever
In this state of perfect ignorance, new-born
To these familiar conditions that will once more
Exalt the heart in breaking it. Come close.
No atlas could describe the distances that sound –
The train, the gust among the tiles and attics –
Offers us for nothing as it fades, the wind
Into itself, the train into its schedule – an express
Importantly imagining the north for those
Who long to go or dare to stay or never

Think of going anywhere at all. Come close.
What business can it be of ours
To feel this way, as though both honoured
And arraigned, to have to give this sound
That might be nothing but the wind
Our tribute of attention till it's gone?

On the Toon

O fairest of the northern waters, river-god, great Tyne, I asked,
Flow through this language now, hydrate the tongue
Afresh, abolish drought and thirst
And let me drink you in to learn
The meaning of our history, and what must be.
Send me a guide from your deep source,
A water-sprite, a river-girl, to go with me.
'The clue you're looking for at thirteen down,'
She said, 'is river-stairs, and learning that
Will cost you. Mine's a turquoise WKD.'
I looked up. There she sat along the bar
In the unmoving reaches of the afternoon
Among the far-gone gadgies in the Crown Posada,
Bold as brass with long black hair, green eyes,
A tiny dress of shifting emerald and jet.
I put the paper down and fetched her drink
And as she raised it to her lips it seemed
We stood beside the Tyne by night, no moon,
A black tide licking past, ourselves alone.
A boat was waiting, moored beneath the stairs.
She led me down, took up the oar, and as we stood
Upright, *traghetto*-style, she swung us out
Beneath the great arch of an unknown bridge
And on into the secret Hell of Tyne.
First came a labyrinth of flooded passageways

With dead men labouring waist-deep in ice
To win the coal that never reached the light.
I saw them crushed between the jaws of tunnels
Only to unearth themselves and then resume
Their labours with a passion whose futility
They knew but would not bow to. No one spoke.
As we moved off, the echo of their picks came
After us a little way until the stream grew broad again
And steered us to a subterranean Sargasso,
The breaker's yard of all the ironclads the Tyne
Had launched for the engagements at Tsushima,
Jutland and the rest. Among the showers of sparks
The welders moved like surgeons, opening
The rusted ribs of battleships still glowing red
From their exploded magazines. Released
Into the smoky air, the drowned men sealed belowdecks
Slid and flopped along the quays as though alive.
Then silent gangs with carts would haul away
These levies to augment Golgotha's pyramids.
'What does this mean?' I asked my guide. 'Bad faith,'
She said, 'to know and not remember; to remember
In a lie; to claim to want the lost world back. Bad faith
Can have no history, only sentiment.' She could have been
A girl from Scotswood, Byker, Wallsend, Shields,
And yet she said these things. Then she slipped off
Her tall red shoes. 'Massage my feet,' she ordered
While our vessel slid among the burnt-out staithes
And over reefs of sunken cars where twockers
Gazed back disbelievingly as fish went stitching
Deftly through the sockets of their eyes. 'We're nearly there –

Although you're not exactly dressed for clubbing.'
'Smart but casual,' I said. 'Aye, in your dreams.
Stay close, say nowt and dee what I dee, right?'
A wall of smoke arose before us, warehouse windows
Speaking bursts of flame as wooden tenements
Consumed themselves and everyone inside,
While firestorms tore down the city's spires
And night ran red and black and gold
As in a biblical comeuppance. Vast
Explosions in the riverbed threw gouts
Of mud and bones around us, yet the girl betrayed
No fear, but brought us to a cobbled ramp
That seemed to tunnel upwards through the fire,
And at its head a pair of vast red doors
Stood open, guarded by a triple-headed bouncer,
All immaculate in black, who chewed his wads
With the ferocity of Alex Ferguson.
'We're on the list,' she said. He waved us in.
Beyond, there lay a wilderness of mirrorwork
And false lights framing ever more exclusive rooms.
The whole place sweated heartless noise, to which
Dog-headed dancing-girls performed
In leotards of black and white, while slabs of lard
In dandruffed suits rewarded them with absolute
Unsmiling concentration, feeding powder
Up their ruined noses as a timeless duty
Princes of the city deign to undertake. So here's
Where money came to waste itself. 'Let's stick
To lemonade,' she said. 'It took them centuries
Of violent integrity to bring

Geordismo to perfection: here's the fruit,
They like to claim, of all that grim endeavour:
Samurai of self-indulgent crap, who bloom
Like cherry-blossom: so. Now let them die.'
On giant screens by the Olympic pool of schnapps
The match was on – was that Gigg Lane? – but
No one watched, since even here at Pleasure Central
Everybody knew the game was up: tonight
Was next time as foretold, tonight was fire.
And as I thought this, flames burst from the pumps
And lard-men's mouths, a final utterance
That kept the faith with all that proud extremity
And had no breath to waste on content after all.

Canto II

'We've seen enough. Now take my hand and run.'
She led me up a granite spiral in the dark
Pursued by screams and smoke, produced a key
And turned it in a cobwebbed lock and let us
Out into a graveyard in the dawn. We sat there
Smoking reefers on the doorstep of the crypt
Of some forgotten liberal benefactor,
Watching the sunrise come up Westgate Hill
Like one more too-familiar promise made
To all those dwellers in the sky whose promised streets
Have fallen off the map of possibility.
'So what have you to say to them?' she asked
And gestured at this city of the poor, whose life and death

Among the towers and tombs seemed interchangeable.
I shook my head and she shook hers and said,
'If nothing else, let dreams be competent. If not
Don't be surprised to see the Swastika take root
Among these boneyards fed on disappointment.'
Then as her sentence ended we arrived
By Cowen's monument. 'It was from here,' she said,
The citizens of Newcastle drove Mosley's thugs
Clean off the street. As for the BNP, I've shat 'em.'
She walked me on along the southern edge
Of Grainger Town towards a secret library,
And as I entered I became a book, half-sealed
With smoke, high on a shelf beside the dome
Of that great reading room. I knew the simple fact
That I spent decades unconsulted meant
That there were those below who eyed me jealously
For pulping. From inside the volume next to me
She said, 'And this is what it's like to be
The general good – neglected first and then
Uncomprehended, finally despised. It takes
Less than a lifetime to renew the ignorance
This public mind was built here to dispel.
Now tell me this, whose interest is served
When people can no longer concentrate but find
Their history's best left to the eccentric few
To whom no one need listen? *Cui bono* then?
Who owns the angel at the gate who bids us leave
The earthly paradise of print?' . . . 'Now, pet,
Yer cannat answer that,' the beggarwoman said,
Upon her throne of rags in Charlotte Square,

A hag of sixty holding court among her favourites,
The Gulf War veteran, the methylated Irishman,
The dead-eyed gluey couple with the dog.
All rose and spoke in chorus at her sign:
'See, Fenkle Street was Fennel Street and fennel is
A vegetable sacred to Apollo, god of light
And reason. He it is who animates the mind
To build the city as his monument, set noble curves
Along its hills, see justice done in arch and pediment,
Cut stone that stores the light like lamps, and raise
High windows for the guardians of sense.
Of course the likes of us could only ever be
The citizens of edge and underside,
Cartographers of Grainger Town's decay
From the Enlightenment by way of two world wars
Into the grip of cheque cashiers and glum arcades
Where those with next to nothing give it back
In coin or else in kind upstairs. We speak the truth
And for our knowledge we are flayed alive
Like Marsyas, today and every day.' With this
They raised their cans in tribute and were gone.
I sought my guide along Back Stowell Street
And found the poets' Tower open to the rain.
The time ran on so fast a winter night
Had fallen as I reached St James's Park,
Whose pitiable interregnum stretched
Unhindered to infinity. The lights were out
But slipping through a turnstile I could sense
An eerie glow, and when I reached the pitch
I saw that this was caused by freezing fires

That leaked from all the tombs crammed in
Beneath that sacred turf, some sealed, some with their lids
Rived off, as though grave-robbers searched
For pieces of the past that they could sell,
As if the spirit were a thing. A corpse stood up
Behind his stone and showed his scarf: 'I wore this
Man and boy,' he said, 'since first my father fetched me
To the match among the thousands, where I learned
To praise the arts of Gallagher and Milburn and the rest.
For here was the ground of our being: here!
But someone has been selling off our dreams.
I cannot sleep. Will you release me from my bond?'
I did his bidding, donned the scarf, and once more
Fled in search of my lost guide, the river-girl.
But now her face appeared on posters everywhere,
As missing child and teenage runaway, one face
For all those we have carelessly mislaid, the photographs
Dissolving as I followed where they led,
Until beside a muddy tributary I found
A locked-in boozer called The Sacrifice.
The iron door swung open at my knock.

Canto III

Inside, a Cyclops with an attitude
Gave me a narrow look and weighed a pool cue
Thoughtfully. 'Why is it called The Sacrifice?' I asked.
'Depends who's asking, pal,' he said, and smiled
At all his radgie fellow revellers

Who nodded to a steely one-chord motorik
And wore their thirsty heads beneath their arms
Like honours claimed in some unceasing war
In which it seemed the enemy tonight was me.
'No, leave him, Poly,' said a voice I almost knew.
The Naiad's older sister stood behind the bar
Dispensing speed and snakebite to the crowd,
Clan-mother to the dead, Medusa-haired
With tiny spitting snakes in black and white.
She handed me a Ziploc and a pint and said,
'This is the very bottom of the night, the last
Redoubt of proletarian bacchanal.
It's where the Fat Slags get the jump on Dionysos,
Rend him limb from limb, then fall asleep
And come the foul-tongued dawn remember nowt
But feel they might have spoken out of turn.
This is a place of endings-up. Your missing guide
Might well have come to grief down here,
Had she not chosen otherwise. Her disappearance
Was a test. Go out the back. You'll find her there.'
Then as I stepped outside into the dark
The pub descended like a lift into the earth
And I could see across the snowy ground
The naiad beckoning impatiently. The tide
Had filled the muddy ditch, so we cast off
Into the blizzard's freezing dark. I put my hand
Upon her arm. She turned and stared at me
Till I removed it. 'All I meant,' I said,
'Was that I do not even know your name.
Who can you be, to wake such fearful care

That I've pursued you to the back of night?'
'I have no name, although you know me well.
My name, you see, is all the town might yet become.
Now watch again to learn if night will end
Or if this underworld of history must be
The grave and sum of all the labour and the love
The ordinary citizens have given here.'
And as she spoke, a curving line of light appeared
And we sped upstream on the tide to pass
Beneath the eye that blinked for us, then swung to rest
To let the early walkers cross the Tyne.
It seemed the day must be some kind of festival,
So many passed and waved to see our little craft
Commanded by the river-girl. Then, looking back,
I saw it was a fleet they welcomed in,
The tall romance of ocean-going sails we seemed
To herald, hundreds crowding from the globe,
Swan-sure and rigged like promises,
To moor along the packed sea-thirsty quays.
The day was fine. The early sun struck galleries
And concert halls, the courts and prison vans alike.
It reached the weather-vanes and tower blocks
And made the walkers in the canyons by the quays
Stare up past empty offices into a sky
That for this hour looked like common property.
All this the water-engine of the Tyne sustained.
We gazed on through the arch of the great bridge,
Beyond the city to the double springs
Where we begin and re-begin, in work and love –
Or so it seemed, borne on that bracing tide of light

And possibility, whose name I think was Paradise,
Since for a moment that was what I seemed to hear
The gathered host declare as one free city-state
Of equal citizens who served the common good.
And then the word was spoken and the crowd
Moved on into ten thousand conversations
And the faces I had seen along the way emerged
A moment and then blended with the rest.
Now while I had been gazing, she had moored
Where we set out and so we climbed the steps
Into the ordinary day, where all the girls like her
Came out to sport their finery and claim
Their portion of the pleasures of the Town.
'You mustn't think that we've arrived,' she said.
'That place waits in the permanent conditional
That's yet to find its time. Time I was gone as well.'
She kissed me on the cheek. 'Take care now, pet.'
She smiled and stepped into the crowd
And disappeared, and all the jostling girls
Were river-girls, and she was all of them.
My eyes grew cloudy then. I felt my way
Towards the Crown Posada, where I sat
Once more inside the shade of afternoon
And tried to grasp the vision while it fled,
Though all I had about me was a biro
From the bookies and a *Chronicle* to write on. O
Great Tyne, I was unworthy of the task.
I lacked the gifts required to convey
The terror and the pity and the hope
I witnessed on my night out on the Toon.

But here it is. So pick the bones from that. 'I think
We need another tense for dreaming in,' I said,
Which made an old drunk shake his head and smile.
And if we dreamed? I couldn't say, but caught
The barman's eye and turned to thirteen down.

Acknowledgements

Agenda, *Art World*, *Black Box Manifold*, *Cardinal Points*, *Cimarron Review*, *The Forward Book of Poetry*, *Manchester Review*, *Granta*, *Holocaust Memorial Day*, the *Irish Times*, *Other Poetry*, *Poetry London*, *Poetry Review*, the *Spectator*, the *Times Literary Supplement*, *Warwick Review*.

A number of these poems appeared in *Night Train*, with pictures by Birtley Aris (Flambard, 2009).

The version of 'Le Bâteau Ivre' was commissioned by the Newcastle Centre for the Literary Arts.

'On the Toon' was commissioned by Newcastle upon Tyne Literary and Philosophical Society.

The author is grateful to the Northern Rock Foundation for the 2007 Writers' Award, which enabled him to devote time to the completion of this book.

NOTE

Cahiers du Cinema. Karl Malden does not in fact appear in *The Battle of the Bulge*. But clearly he should.